PIERRE-AUGUSTE RENOIR

ANTHONY BOSMAN

1900

Pierre-Auguste Renoir

BARNES & NOBLE, INC.

NEW YORK

Publishers • Booksellers • Since 1873

Editor: Anthony Bosman
Translation: Corry van Alphen
Published in the United States in 1962
by Barnes & Noble, Inc., 105 Fifth Avenue, New York 3, N.Y.
© 1961 and printed in Holland by The Ysel Press Ltd, Deventer

PIERRE-AUGUSTE RENOIR

When Renoir was twenty-one years old, he went to practise painting at the studio of Charles Gleyre, having saved enough money by painting imitation stained-glass windows. Gleyre was a mediocre Swiss artist, who showed himself once or twice a week to his pupils, amongst whom were Claude Monet, Alfred Sisley, and Jean Frédérique Bazille—in order to correct their work in the manner of the classical spirit of Ingres. Gleyre, full of contempt for artists like Diaz, Jongkind, and Corot, who were admired by his pupils, said to Renoir one day, "One does not paint for pleasure," to which Renoir retorted, "If painting were no pleasure to me, I would not paint." The answer is characteristic of Renoir. If his work was appreciated, he had a feeling of exultation that could hardly be equaled. He was also an artist who derived an inexhaustible joy from all facets of life. These two motives were indissolubly united, and it is to their combined power that the richness of Renoir's art owes its existence.

Renoir was a warmhearted and intensely alive man. His heart was drawn to the sun, so much so that he once said, "Why should one paint snow, that leprosy of nature?" For him, the world consisted of sun and light, of the voluptuousness of a woman's body—which should, he said, be painted as if it were a beautiful fruit. And so he did, in a bold, free, and lyrical manner, even when he returned, in the years 1883-1887, to classical design, with concentration on linear structure and monumental form. His landscapes and urban scenes, his still lifes and portraits, are as thoroughly steeped in sunshine as his nudes. All these works sing a song of life—carefree, unpreoccupied, tasting enjoyment to the full. Renoir is the absolute antithesis of the tortured Vincent van Gogh, and also of many other contemporaries, such as the misanthropic Manet, the cynically detached Toulouse-Lautrec, the aloof, unbending Cézanne. It is as if all pain and sorrow, all problems have passed him by, as if Life has met him with open arms.

But the opposite is the case. During his early years, which were not easy financially, he is described as an easy-going, friendly fellow, gay, cheerful, and fond of the girls. He was an artist who surrounded himself with kindred spirits and took pleasure in parties on boats, in dance halls, and in the garden of his studio in Montmartre. Later, after he had married his model Aline Charigot in 1881 and his first son, Pierre, had been born in 1885, he turned into a typical French paterfamilias who works from eight in the morning till five in the afternoon, is well looked after by his wife, and goes to bed at an early hour, perhaps after a game of dominoes. The only unusual feature of the household was that the maids had to serve as models for him—were, in fact, selected for the quality of their skin in sunlight. In 1882 the first symptoms of rheumatism appeared after Renoir had pneumonia (from which he convalesced in Algiers). For twelve years the illness was only noticeable at times, but then its grip became ever stronger and more devastating. In vain he sought a cure by taking the waters at Aix-les-Bains. The rheumatism penetrated every fiber of his body and made him a helpless cripple. Several operations were performed on his hands, his knees, and his feet, but they brought him little relief. Renoir was twisted and bent over by the terrible disease. He had to drag himself on crutches, and when, in 1911, even this was no longer possible, he used a wheel chair.

But whatever rheumatism may have done to his body, Renoir's love of life survived. He spoke of himself as "a remarkably lucky fellow" because he could still handle a brush, even if it had to be inserted by someone else in the deformed fist that was once his hand. There were times of despair when he thought of giving up painting. But when a new model showed up he once more went into ecstasies and with that one brush, which he had to swish through turpentine every time he wished to apply a new color, he extolled the beauty of form, color, and light. His vision was undiminished although his brush stroke had lost some of its firmness. No one would expect to find behind the paintings created at that time a man almost crumpled up by a deadly disease. His works radiated the same joy and vitality as formerly. *That* is, humanly speaking, the greatest marvel of Renoir.

Renoir was born on the 25th day of February, 1841, at Limoges, the son of a tailor with a small business who had the greatest difficulty in earning his daily bread and who moved to Paris in 1845, hoping to do better there. Pierre-Auguste, as the future artist was named, soon had to help support the family, and when he was thirteen he was apprenticed to a decorator in a china factory. The reason for this choice by his parents is obvious. Limoges was a town where from the end of the fifteenth century until Louis XIV the art of enameling flourished and where from 1736 onward porcelain factories appeared one after the other. A child who filled his exercise books with drawings and showed talent was naturally sent to a china factory, where he not only learned a trade but also earned money.

For five long years little Pierre painted china, beginning at a wage of a halfpenny a dozen. He started with flowers and finally arrived at a portrait of Marie Antoinette which brought him fourpence each. The factory did not flourish even though the owner placed a counterfeit Sèvres trademark on the china intended for export. When a way was devised to decorate china mechanically, Pierre lost his job.

However, the value of these five years for the seventeen-year-old boy was not inconsiderable. He had five years' experience in the quick and accurate handling of his brush and a great knowledge of rococo decoration. Moreover, his factory was situated near the Louvre, which he visited during his meal times.

Young Renoir found a new job in the studio of a fan-painter. On the fans he painted gallant scenes in imitation of great eighteenth-century artists such as Watteau, Boucher, and Fragonard. The "Baby Rubens," as he was nicknamed, not only copied but also studied in the Louvre the colors and brush techniques of the great virtuosos of the rococo period, for whose pictures, full of playfulness and the joy of life, he felt an affinity.

The basis of Renoir's art was laid in those years, and in later years he acknowledged, in conversations with the art dealer Vollard (who secretly made notes of them) that he owed his sense of the plastic qualities of the female form and of clear, almost transparent colors, to Watteau, Fragonard, and Boucher. The elements of Renoir's work can certainly be traced to these artists.

Through Watteau and Boucher he reached back to Rubens, whose work had influenced both of them. Although in the rococo period the tempestuousness of Rubens was softened and transformed into an idyllic and dreamlike art, yet Rubens' love of the female form and the coloring of the nude was transmitted to Renoir and given new substance by him. A spiritual affinity exists between Rubens and Renoir. Both work with an Olympian passion for form and color and are able to capture and hold the warmth of life. Both know how to retain the impact of a first impression and to combine it with eternal values, which are the essence of art. Their works are dedicated to Life, but in such a way that the material joins with the spiritual in a single paean of praise—with Rubens, tempestuous and daring; with Renoir, more reserved and contemplative. It might be put thus: Rubens was the conqueror, but Renoir was his heir.

When Renoir left the fan-painter's studio, money was still a serious problem, and this time he found a job with a maker of window shutters who supplied missionaries with imitation stained-glass windows, so that a poor building in the tropics would be given the appearance of a church. The Adoration of the Magi and the Assumption of the Virgin Mary were favorite subjects. Renoir did these so well that he earned enough to put money aside to learn painting properly at last. (He had already taken lessons for some terms at the School of Fine Arts.)

Finally, in 1862, he entered the studio of Gleyre—which proved to have two advantages: the infrequency of the visits of the master and the friendship of Monet, Sisley, and Bazille.

Monet has said that he could only bear the studio for two weeks and then took his three friends out to work in the open air. This does not, however, tally with the facts. The young artists only went outside to paint, the following spring, when Gleyre had to close his studio for lack of money to pay the models. This meant for Renoir and his friends a farewell to the academic tradition and freedom to enjoy the work of the artists admired at that moment.

In the case of Renoir, these were Courbet, the realist, perhaps Delacroix, the romantic and the founder of impressionism, and Diaz, a sentimentalist of the Barbizon school.

In 1863 another artist was attracting attention: Édouard Manet. The person chiefly responsible for the interest in Manet was none other than the Emperor Napoleon III, and this is how it happened. The Emperor visited the Annual Exhibition of the Salon des Beaux Arts before it was opened to the public and requested that the rejected works be shown to him. When he had seen a number of them, he expressed the opinion that the rejected paintings were just as good as those that had been accepted and ordered that all the rejected works should be exhibited in a Salon des Réfusés. It was, however, not so much a love of art which led the Emperor to make this decision as the large number of protests which had been received against the decisions of the jury. Moreover, this was his chance to play a trick on De Nieuwerkerke, the Superintendent of the Beaux Arts and Curator of the Imperial Museum, who was the lover of the Princess Mathilda.

This exhibition of rejected paintings created a scandal on account of Manet's now-famous picture "The Picnic" (*Le Déjeuner sur l'herbe*), then called "The Bath" (*Le Bain*). It was considered disgraceful that an artist should have the temerity to paint a nude woman in a wood, between two men who were clothed. When the Empress Eugénie visited the exhibition, she pretended not to see the picture. The Emperor contemplated it in silence and then said, "That picture is an insult to chastity!"

This meant the end of the Salon des Réfusés, and there was never a second one. The young artists, however, had become acquainted with Manet's work, which created a deep impression on them by its striking realism and the daring with which a theme of Giorgione had been transposed into their own time.

Manet set an example which Renoir did not immediately follow. Courbet still remained his ideal and his master. A certain encounter was to prove very important. One day as he sat painting in the Forest of Fontainebleau, a man with a wooden leg approached and, after examining Renoir's canvas, said: "I am also an artist; my name is Diaz. The drawing is not bad, but why on earth do you paint everything so black?"

Diaz, one of the artists Renoir admired, was able to persuade him to change his somber colors for fresher, brighter ones. He even opened an account for him with his own color dealer and gave him advice. This event proved decisive; the use of lighter colors led toward a new vision. Courbet retained his influence over Renoir for a few more years, as is clearly shown in the picture "Diana Hunting" *(Diane chasseresse),* painted in 1867, but in that landscape there appears for the first time a transition toward a new manner of looking at the world.

For the time being, however, Renoir had no idea of imitating impressionism and its techniques. Nor was this the case with Monet, Sisley, and Pissarro. Their work shows, like that of Renoir, a new awareness of a fresh vision without its being attained. The tie with the great predecessors, such as Courbet and Corot, and with the older contemporary, Manet, remains.

Yet the work of Renoir done in the years before 1870—the year war broke out between France and Germany—repeatedly shows landscapes and river scenes in which the vibration of the light leads him to use a technique of small spots of color which, combined, create the impression of the mobility of flowing water. This is especially marked in the case of the bathing place "La Grenouillère on the Seine" *(La Grenouillère),* which dates from 1868-69. Yet in those same years he painted works like "Freighters on the Seine" *(Chalands sur la Seine),* which are very far removed from any impressionistic vision.

Renoir and Monet worked together a great deal during this time and their development was equally gradual, although Monet was more daring and Renoir apparently did not wish to burn all his boats behind him. The war put an end to their working together. Monet and Pissarro went to England, and Sisley, an Englishman, also left. Monet spent some time in the Netherlands before crossing to England. Renoir became a soldier. General Douay offered him his protection, but Renoir refused to accept it. Fortune favored him: he went as a cuirassier (a cavalryman wearing a cuirass—leather armor) to Bordeaux, later to Marseilles, and led a fairly peaceful existence which afforded him opportunities to paint. The portraits of Captain Darras and his wife date from this period—technical master-pieces but without importance for Renoir's development as an artist. This development was resumed after his return to Paris in 1871. There, in the Café Guerbois—the place where before the war those painters who were inspired with regene-rating ideas used to meet—he again met his friends, who ventured to return to Paris when the bloody overthrow and punishment of the Commune were past.

Monet and Pissarro had seen in London the work of Turner, that English artist who, about 1830, converted the effects of atmosphere and light, which he had already made an integral element of his water colors, into oils, and who during the last twenty years of his life depicted visions of light wherein shapes dissolved into an artist's dream in yellow-gold, pale pinks, and ultramarine. The work of Turner, veritably possessed by light, hastened their approach to the thought that light and color are synonymous.

Monet, Pissarro, and Sisley, however, wished to work differ-ently. Not like Turner, intuitively—they considered that too romantic and unscientific—but constructively, by an analysis of color and shadow: the representation of light by small strokes of color from a palette where the colors of the spectrum dominate and complementary colors are used for shadows. This technique went hand in hand with the first principle of im-pressionism: painting should be a direct and spontaneous rendering of that which the eye observes. The visual sensation is to be put on the canvas.

The technical principle of impressionism has an extensive pedigree. It may be traced back to Titian, who depicted light effects by means of spots of color, and to Velázquez and Goya, who sometimes made use of broken colors. Constable utilized adjacent component colors in order to create a total impression

Self-portrait of Renoir, about 35 years old.
(Fogg Art Museum, Cambridge, Mass., U.S.A.)

of a single color. Delacroix, after seeing the works of Constable before the opening of the Paris Salon of 1824, was so deeply impressed by them that he repainted the "Scenes of the Massacre of Chios," intended for that exhibition, in four days, giving them an entirely different appearance by the use of half-tones—applying spots and dabs of primary colors and using tiny brush strokes for details. He wrote down his discoveries in his diary, and these discoveries anticipated impressionism.

There are yet other predecessors, among them the Dutchman Johan Barthold Jongkind, who was able by means of his strong visual memory to paint at home French and Dutch landscapes and harbors in a brilliant, purely impressionistic style of drafts-manship and painting made up of touches of color, from which the spots of color were developed. There is also Manet, who even before 1870, influenced by photography, painted in tonal values—impressionism before its time.

This was the background from which during the 1870's impressionism sprang. Renoir and Monet often worked together in the neighborhood of Argenteuil, on the banks of the Seine, where Monet had gone to live. Together they discovered what had to be manifested, the palette with all the colors of the rainbow, the use of complementary colors, the unavoidable sacrifice of shape and form to the light—and all this permeated by throbbing life. The painting became a song of life and light, the transfiguration of the unlimited vision, the total surrender to the spontaneous impression and the sensual reaction.

Renoir became an impressionist, but not so unreservedly as Monet, who ruthlessly advanced on the chosen path. Renoir went along with impressionism insofar as it enhanced the appreciation of life, but he was unwilling to sacrifice the beauty and solidity of shape and form. He therefore did not develop steadily in one direction like Monet and Pissarro, but was now advancing, now turning back to the traditional. In his landscapes one can see how the light penetrated there as a fluid entity, but he still used in the same picture a combination of new and old techniques.

His first large work, "The Loge" *(La Loge)*, which was displayed at the first exhibition of the impressionists in 1874, shows this duality very clearly. It is traditional in that the canvas was painted in the studio from models, not in the open air; the brush work is impressionistic and the color is clear and sonorous, but the black abominated by the impressionists is not lacking.

It was not long, however, before the impressionistic vision invaded the realm of portraiture; the subject then became atmosphere, color, and light rather than humanity. Renoir reached out to seize life as it is lived in Montmartre, at the Moulin de la Galette, with the Sunday crowds of people eating, drinking, and dancing. "The Moulin de la Galette" is a feast of vibrating color, sublime in the presentation of the figures and imbued with the spirit of carefree jollity. But even in this picture, which may be regarded as a masterpiece of the impressionistic Renoir, he still respects volume and does not sacrifice it to light.

From 1876 on, a series of ravishing impressionistic works are created. "The Swing" *(La Balançoire)*, painted before the "Moulin de la Galette," showed the same use of color. "Girl Reading" *(La Liseuse)* is wholly impressionistic in technique and shows a delightful mastery of craftsmanship, so much so that the face seems to radiate light. "The First Evening Out" *(La Première Sortie)* is a second "The Loge" but different in subject and technique. This time it is not the beauty of the woman that is the center of attraction but the youthful anticipation of the young girl, whose figure forms a contrast with the sketchy figures of other members of the audience at the side. Finally, "The Luncheon of the Boating Party at Bougival" *(Le Déjeuner des canotiers)*, which dates from 1881, is one of the most beautiful Renoirs, not only because of its rich and warmly alive coloring, but also because each one of the persons pictured is a living entity, united with the others in the bounty and exuberance of a sunny summer's day on the banks of the Seine.

By this time Renoir had many admirers. His daily bread was assured by the art dealers Durand-Ruel and by the many portrait commissions he received. When, in 1878, he painted Madame Charpentier and her two little daughters in a large group portrait, the publisher Charpentier introduced him into society and his success was enormous.

It is probable that the conventional portraits like that of the Charpentier family brought the artist to a realization of more intrinsic values. A journey to Italy in 1881 was a great stimulus in this direction. He was confronted by the classic masters in the museums, which he visited with a real passion. Raphael and the frescoes of Pompeii made him realize what is lost in the sacrifice by impressionists of form and outline. These works awakened a desire and ambition in him for an art more substantial than impressionism, a dissatisfaction which had been latent in him and had sometimes manifested itself by intruding itself into the impressionist vision. Now it asserted itself irresistibly.

Renoir did not stand alone in his discontent with the impressionist vision and technique, the specialization of vision, the evaporation of the subject. There was Cézanne, who had never been a doctrinaire impressionist and strove more and more to render the structure of things in terms of color. There was also Seurat, who carried the impressionist theories of color to their culmination by analyzing each color with scientific accuracy and applying the component parts in tiny spots of pure pigments on his canvas, but for whom the pictorial structure was always the chief thing.

The revolt against impressionism may be said to have begun in 1884—ten years after the impressionists had called attention to themselves with their first exhibition. Renoir was a precursor of that revolt, for his famous "The Blonde Bather" *(Baigneuse blonde)*, which was formerly in the possession of Sir Kenneth Clark, may have been painted during his Italian journey (1881) while he was very much under the influence of Raphael. The striking linear and substantial qualities link this picture with "The Umbrellas," in which a similar striving is evident—with, in addition, an unmistakable classical appeal.

The feast of color and light is over. Now the color is applied smoothly; his palette contains ochres, cobalt blues, greens, and black. Linear structure, volume, and a harmonious composition constructed in accordance with the classical ideal, are the principal elements.

"Almost according to pattern" might be said of the picture "The Bathers" *(Les Grandes Baigneuses)*, from the Tyson collection, which Renoir began in 1883-84 and finished in 1885. It cannot be without intent that he adopted the classical subject from a bas-relief of the seventeenth-century sculptor François Girardon, thereby placing himself outside of his period and outside of the technique cultivated by the impressionists. In this picture Renoir attempted to create something divorced from time, and many were the sketches he made for it, ever striving for perfection of line. The result was a work of great, but somewhat formal, beauty, captivating in its play of line and form, plastic in its sculptural power in spite of the absence of shadow.

For almost three years Renoir worked on this painting. He began with drawings of bathers, numerous drawings, in which he concentrated on the human figure. He tried to delineate everything in contour, which the impressionists refused to acknowledge, since an enclosing line was in contradiction with

17

their principle of light uniting every part and bringing it to vibrating life. Monet and all other orthodox impressionists regarded the line as a prison in which one attempted to incarcerate nature. As a result they did very little drawing. But for Renoir a definite contour was the way to arrive at perfection. It was as if he knew the words of Ingres: "The power of expression in painting requires a very great knowledge of drawing, for the expression cannot be good if it is not formulated with absolute accuracy.... One cannot reach the utmost precision except through the most certain talent for drawing." So Renoir practiced drawings for two or three years before he felt secure enough to transfer them to oil paintings.

Earlier, Renoir had done some drawings, occasionally with pencil, sometimes with ink, but usually with pastels because with pastels it was easier to capture the impressionist play of light. A fortunate event led him to do even more drawing than usual: the founding of a weekly paper *La Vie moderne,* published by Georges Charpentier, his patron. He made portraits of important people for this journal and also illustrated the short stories written by his brother Edmont. This was after 1879, but in his earlier period, from about 1875 on, he had made a number of pastels of young girls which have the fascinating qualities of what might be called the blossom time of Renoir's impressionistic period. The palpitating life of light is captured in the pastel colors, and moreover he has caught the nature of the young girl in her prime as a woman, with all her charm and mystery. Even in the black-and-white reproductions one can feel the force of the colors in the brilliant contrasts of light and dark.

In the drawings from after 1881, when the bathers begin to appear, and when pencil, crayon (black and red), and pen replace the pastels in an attempt to depict woman in contour, we see another Renoir: a Renoir inspired by the classical

18   *(continued on page 73)*

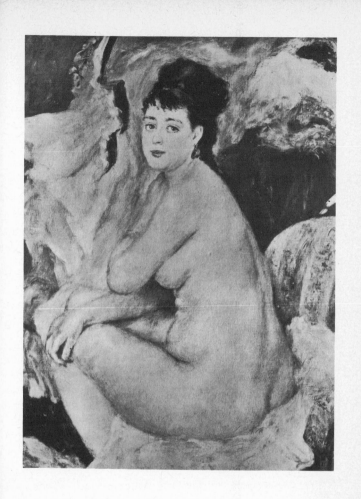

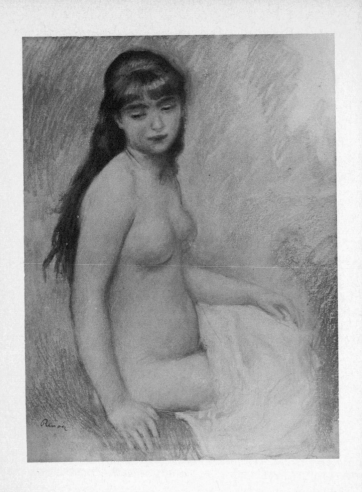

43

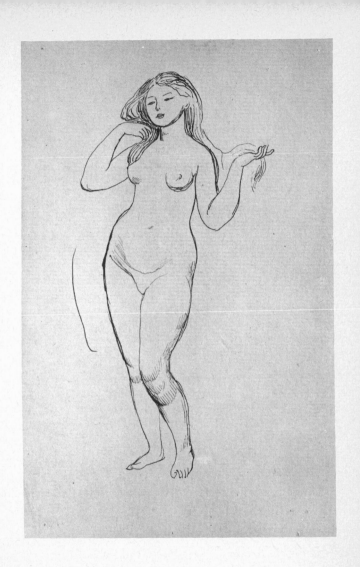

50

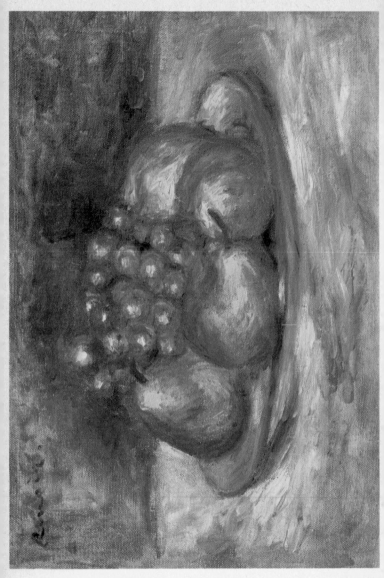

example of Raphael and Ingres, but expressing himself with great freedom and quite in his own period. The numerous studies of the bathers reveal the painter searching for the strictest simplicity—while retaining a quality of aliveness—and striving for linear harmony. One can also see an increasing concentration on composition in his drawings as he moves some figures into the background and focuses on the three bathers who are to dominate the painting. Slowly his own conception takes form and the bas-relief of Girardon gradually vanishes until Renoir arrives at his own creation—just as Manet's "Picnic" had been his own re-creation of Giorgione's "Rural Concerts," which hangs in the Louvre.

Rarely has an artist created such a noble work in a time of crisis, for so one may designate the period of revolt against impressionism from about 1884 to the end of the century. He became wholly preoccupied with contour, after the examples of Raphael and Ingres had made their impact upon his nature, which longed to revel in the enjoyment of the fullness of life in spite of the tendency, repeatedly shown in his work, toward the classical tradition.

It is as though Renoir at this time purposely confined himself in a classical strait jacket: a veritable explosion of light and color was followed by the utmost discipline of line, a thin application of color so that the brush stroke disappeared, and finally a cooling of his inner warmth.

Renoir's perfect achievement in "The Bathers" was a success because he had set himself a classical, timeless problem, but there were difficulties when he had to deal with subjects in the costumes and surroundings of his own time. Only in those instances where he could transpose the subject into a stylized classical vision can one speak of a strict linear style and a painting technique which scarcely betrays the touch of the brush.

Some pictures of this period display a return to the play of light and to occasional brush strokes, indicating that now and then Renoir escaped from the aim which he had set for himself.

It is at this time that he was closely associated with Cézanne, whom he visited in Aix-les-Bains, and with whom he worked at La Rouche-Guyon and at l'Estaque in 1887. Renoir, however, went his own way; Cézanne could not solve Renoir's problems for him. Nevertheless, Renoir enjoyed the company of a congenial spirit who also had left impressionism for a more lasting art. While Cézanne arrived at an entirely new form of design which would prove to be of decisive significance for the development of the plastic arts (cubism), Renoir could do nothing else but return to classicism, which did not eadl forward toward a new vision.

The year 1890 or thereabouts may be denoted as the turning point for Renoir. He now attempted a compromise between classicism and impressionism, but his evolution was slow. He again went traveling, this time to the Netherlands, where he found Rembrandt joyless and cared to remember only the glowing yellow girl with the chicken dangling from her girdle. Then on to Spain, where El Greco, Velázquez, and Goya aroused his admiration by their discoveries in the realm of color, light, and shadow.

Before returning to the Chateau des Brouillards in Montmartre, to his wife, his seven-year-old son Pierre (Jean was to be born the following year, in 1893), and the two servant girl-models, he had observed in the art of Velázquez how that artist modeled with light and nuances of tone and thereby achieved a strong spontaneity of presentation—also how this Spanish artist of the seventeenth century combined a kind of impressionistic method with a firmness of form. During the course of several years Renoir succeeded in attaining a similar synthesis, one in his own manner and completely of his own time.

Photograph of Renoir, about 1905.

Renoir rediscovered impressionism, but he now used it entirely differently from his application of it in the 1870's. There is no evidence of a retreat from impressionism, but in the nineties he knew how to combine it with solidity of form. He abandoned the isolating contour, but did not give up firm construction, which gradually took shape by means of long-drawn-out strokes of the brush. Light no longer dissolved the forms, but modeled them with its touch, supple and full of grace, transparent and radiant.

More and more Renoir approached that joy of living which had always been inside him but now burst forth unrestrained, in compelling nudes and intimately warm portraits of his second son, Jean, with or without the company of his favorite model and servant Gabrielle, whom he painted innumerable times as a bather.

It was in 1894 that Renoir, at the age of fifty-three, suffered his first serious attacks of rheumatism, and from that year onwards his physical condition got worse. Four years later his illness was so aggravated that he began to take the waters at Aix-les-Bains and Bourbonne-les-Bains. His joy of living, however, did not diminish. In 1897, at Essoyes, he even dared to learn to ride a bicycle, which resulted in a broken arm. In 1899 during the treatment at Aix-les-Bains he remarked, "If the cure bores me too much, I shall follow it up with Gabrielle."

The rheumatism continued and his movements became more and more difficult. He always spent his winters in the South, but he returned to Essoyes, in Burgundy, where he had bought a house during the summer of 1898, and to Paris, which he could not do without. He had not had any financial cares for a long while; the art dealers Durand-Ruel and Ambroise Vollard took care of that. His works were even sold in America.

Thus came the turn of the century. Renoir, now fifty-nine, painted his children, especially Jean, and later on Claude

Self-portrait of Renoir, with white hat, 69 years old.
(Paris, Durand-Ruel)

("Coco"), who was born in 1901, and of course Gabrielle, and his wife's niece. During 1905 he established himself at Cagnes, a village situated between Nice and Cannes, lying high up in the hills. It is there that Renoir, more and more crippled by his rheumatism, delivered himself up entirely to the sensual delight which painting was to him.

Renoir was now sixty-four. His body might be tortured, but when seated before his easel his spirit knew only the rapture of form and color. Not a trace of his disease was to be seen in his works. His pictures became more captivating than ever, and sang an unending anthem of rich harmonies. He had to use crutches in order to be able to move at all. In 1910 even this became impossible and he became entirely helpless and had to be carried from his bed to his wheel chair. His hands were twisted out of shape and the nails of his warped fingers penetrated the palm of his hand, which had to be protected by bandages.

Yet this man was able in such circumstances to create a work which expressed sheer joy of life and living. His body was stiff, almost mummified, painful in all parts, a serious bronchitis made breathing an anguish, but Renoir painted on with that one brush fixed in his hand, not by moving his hand, for that was no longer possible, but by moving his arm. On the canvas appeared nudes in delightful roundness, radiating and permeated by sunshine; the landscape around the house La Colette, glowing and magnificently alive; and many still lifes showing sun-baked fruits and blossoms.

But that was not all. During those last ten years of his life Renoir attained that for which he had striven all his life. From 1890 on, he had traveled the road to sculptural plastic values, which had to materialize without accentuated contours, produced by the play of light on the mass of the material. .

Increasingly he started from the mass and generalized the plastic forms. His search was for total harmony, that of his universe, and he sacrificed the incidental to the totality, so that line, tone, and color have a diminished representational function and serve to create a spiritual unity. On account of this, the nude acquired a different significance in the work of the latter years. Formerly the female figure was the center of interest, the nucleus of the picture; now it became part of the landscape and was absorbed in it. The earlier nudes possessed individuality; the later ones were generalized into a kind of still-life quality.

The works of this period were to a high degree lyrical. Richness of coloring flourished as never before. Reds in innumerable shades took a preeminent place. In the very last works of all, in which we should expect to detect fatigue, almost incapacity, hard pinks intrude and predominate, and the beauty of coloring is partly lost.

Until the very last day of his life, December 3, 1919, Renoir continued to paint. After his death several hundreds of canvases were found in his studio at Hautes Cagnes—and this after the art dealers had purchased everything they could get from him, for Renoir had become an esteemed master, who had received the Legion of Honor in 1912. His lifework consisted of more than four thousand pictures, the result of an almost daily toil, which for him was a labor of love and a continuous joy. He *had* to work, and even when he was almost totally incapacitated and often could not hold a brush because of the excruciating pain he could not desist from creating.

Near the end of his career the most extraordinary thing happened: Renoir became a sculptor. It was the dealer Vollard who gave him this idea. But how could Renoir possibly create sculpture with his powerless hands? The astute art dealer provided the means: Renoir could borrow hands, the hands of a young sculptor.

Vollard went to Maillol and laid the problem before him.

Maillol had an assistant, Richard Guino, whom he considered suitable for the work. A young sculptor who did not yet possess his own style, a good craftsman with great adaptability, someone who would never in his own right be a great sculptor. Guino was willing to work with Renoir. Vollard succeeded in persuading Renoir. Have not many sculptures been made by assistants while the sculptor himself has only created a small model, and why should Guino not be able to carry out Renoir's intentions?

Renoir had always had a great feeling for sculpture. In 1907 he had made a medallion of the head of his youngest son Claude ("Coco"), and some months later a bust of him.

The miracle happened: an absolute sympathy and understanding united the spirit of Renoir and the hands of Guino. As Renoir's eldest son, Pierre, has said: "There immediately existed an inner communication between the old master and the young sculptor, sufficiently complete to make communal work a possibility. Renoir led Guino with a small baton in his hand and they understood each other so well that my father scarcely needed to say a word. A simple indication with the baton, an agreeing or disagreeing sound, and the work proceeded quietly." (*Figaro*, October 25, 1934, quoted by Paul Haesaerts in *Renoir Sculptor*.)

That is how the sculpture of Renoir was born. Nineteen works with the aid of Guino, three with the help of Louis Morel, who served the master in the year 1918. Works which vary from eight inches high—the bas-relief "Judgment of Paris"—to "Venus Victorious," which is six feet high. Works which are wholly Renoir's, his creations, although he did not do the actual manual labor. Every smallest detail is a witness to his vision, his ideals, his creative power.

Renoir's sculpture is closely related to his painting, and we may well believe that he experienced it as a kind of culmination, the solidity for which he had always striven in painting now become tangible. Possibly no other artist ever sought tangibility as did Renoir, who experienced a sensual delight in just touching the surface of a painting. Furthermore, he had always longed to achieve a classic monumentality.

But Renoir's Venuses (painted and sculptured) do not emanate solely from classicism; they are permeated by his sensuality, in which there is no desire. His female figures are earthy, fecund in their noble forms; in them the classical element is united with an element of rejuvenation such as we also find in the work of Maillol. The whole of Renoir's rich and intensely alive work constitutes a hymn of the Mediterranean spirit.

LIST OF ILLUSTRATIONS

19 THE LOGE
1874, oil, 31½ × 25 in. Courtauld Institute of Art, London
with permission of the Home House Trustees

20 HEAD OF A YOUNG GIRL
1875, pastel, 19¾ × 15½ in. Durand-Ruel, Paris

21 GIRL READING (La Liseuse), 1876, oil, 18½ × 15 in. Louvre, Paris

22 PORTRAIT OF A YOUNG GIRL WITH HAT
1875-79, pastel, 11¾ × 9½ in. Durand-Ruel, Paris

23 THE MOULIN DE LA GALETTE, Montmartre (detail, left-hand
side)
1876, oil, 52 × 65¾ in. complete painting. Louvre, Paris

24 THE ROSE GARDEN
1870, oil, 15 × 18 in. Private collection, Geneva

25 PATH GOING UP INTO THE HIGH GRASS
1870, oil, 23¼ × 29 in. Louvre, Paris

26 IN THE CAFÉ
1874-75, oil, 13½ × 10¼ in. Rijksmuseum Kröller-Müller,
Otterlo

27 PORTRAIT OF MADAME CHARPENTIER
1877, oil, 19 × 15¾ in. Louvre, Paris

28 GIRL IRONING
Crayon, 18½ × 11½ in. Museum Boymans-Van Beuningen,
Rotterdam

29 THE FIRST EVENING OUT (La Première Sortie)
1876, oil, 25½ × 19¾ in. Tate Gallery, London

30 THE SWING (La Balançoire)
1876, oil, 35¾ × 28 in. Louvre, Paris

31 PORTRAIT OF NINI LOPEZ
 1880, oil, 19 × 15¾ in. Louvre, Paris

32 SKETCH WITH PLAYING CHILDREN (fragment)
 Red and white crayon, 10¾ × 16½ in.
 Museum Boymans-Van Beuningen, Rotterdam

33 THE LUNCHEON OF THE BOATING PARTY AT BOUGIVAL (Le
 Déjeuner des canotiers)
 1881, oil, 50½ × 68 in. Philips Memorial Gallery,
 Washington

34 STUDY FOR THE PORTRAIT OF JULIE MANET WITH HER CAT
 1887, crayon, 24 × 17 in. Collection of Mme. Ernest
 Rouart, Paris

35 THE UMBRELLAS
 1882–83, oil, 71 × 45½ in. National Gallery, London

36 YOUNG WOMAN AGAINST A BLUE BACKGROUND
 1884, oil, 25½ × 21 in. Henri Bernstein collection, Paris

37 HEAD OF A YOUNG GIRL (study for the painting "Girl Reading")
 Red crayon, 12¼ × 9½ in. Private collection, Holland

38 TWO NUDES STANDING
 Crayon and pen, 6¾ × 6 in. Musée de la Ville au Petit Palais,
 Paris

39 ANNA
 1876, oil, 36 × 29 in. Museum of Western Art, Moscow

40 BATHER
 1882–90, pastel, 23¾ × 17¾ in. Durand-Ruel, Paris

41 THE BLONDE BATHER (La Baigneuse blonde)
 1881, oil, 31½ × 25 in. Marlborough Fine Art Ltd (former
 collection Sir Kenneth Clark), London

42 THE BATHERS (Les Grandes Baigneuses)
1887, oil, 45¼×67 in. Carroll S. Tyson, Jr.,
collection, Philadelphia

43 STUDY FOR "THE BATHERS"
One of the many sketches which Renoir made for this
painting. This drawing is a study for the right-hand part
of the canvas.
1884-85, red and black crayon, heightened with white.
34½×20½ in. Durand-Ruel, Paris

44 STANDING NUDE
Crayon, 6¾×4 in. Musée de la Ville au Petit Palais, Paris

45 VENUS (Le Phénomène futur)
1887, pen and ink, 6¾×4½ in. Durand-Ruel, Paris

46 WASHERWOMAN AND CHILD
About 1886, pastel, 31¾×25½ in. Private collection,
Cleveland

47 GABRIELLE WITH JEAN RENOIR
1895, pastel, 25¼×18 in. Durand-Ruel, Paris

48 MOTHERHOOD (Mrs. Renoir with her son Pierre)
1885, red crayon, heightened with white on beige prepared
linen, 35½×28 in. Museum, Strasbourg

49 MOTHERHOOD
1916, bronze, 21¼×9¾×11½ in. Kunsthalle, Bremen

50 SLEEPING GIRL (La Dormeuse)
1897, oil, 32×25 in. Reinhart collection, Winterthur Switz.

51 BATHER ON A ROCK
1892, oil, 31½×25 in. Durand-Ruel, Paris

52 THE JUDGMENT OF PARIS
The shepherd Paris, kneeling with his right leg on the ground, gives the golden apple to Aphrodite, the middle one of the three goddesses, as a token of her being the most beautiful.
1916, bronze, high relief, 29½ × 36 in. Stedelijk Museum, Amsterdam

53 DETAIL OF "THE JUDGMENT OF PARIS" (see 52)
Standing figure

54 DETAIL OF "THE JUDGMENT OF PARIS" (see 52)
Figure at the extreme right

55 THE FRUIT PICKER (probably Renoir's wife)
About 1885, water color, 13½ × 12¼ in. Louvre, Paris

56 LANDSCAPE NEAR L'ETANG DE BERRE, MARTIGUES
1888, pencil and water color, 6½ × 8¾ in. Private collection

57 GIRL WITH EARS OF CORN
1888, oil, 25½ × 21¼ in. Museu de Arte, Sâo Paulo

58 BATHER DRYING HERSELF
Pen and ink. Louvre, Paris

59 GIRL COMBING HER HAIR
1894, oil, 21¼ × 18 in. Robert Lehman collection, New York

60 TWO GIRLS AT THE PIANO
1893, oil, 45¾ × 34¾ in. Louvre, Paris

61 PORTRAIT OF CLAUDE RENOIR ("Coco")
1905-08, oil, 21¾ × 18 in. Museu de Arte, Sâo Paulo

62 TWO YOUNG GIRLS SITTING ON THE GROUND
About 1894, crayon, 16¼ × 12 in. Museum Boymans-Van Beuningen, Rotterdam

63 GIRLS AT THE SEASIDE
1894, oil, 21¾ × 18 in. Durand-Ruel, Paris

64 THE LAUNDRESS (La Lessiveuse)
1917, bronze, 48½ × 52¼ in. Stedelijk Museum, Amsterdam

65 GIRL COMBING HER HAIR (La Toilette)
1910, oil, 21¾ × 18 in. Louvre, Paris

66 STILL LIFE WITH PEARS, APPLES, AND GRAPES
About 1905, oil. Lopez collection, Algiers

67 LANDSCAPE NEAR CAGNES
About 1905, oil. Lopez collection, Algiers

68 VENUS VICTORIOUS
1915-16, bronze, 70¾ × 43¼ in. Museum Boymans-Van Beuningen, Rotterdam

69 BATHER DRYING HERSELF
About 1910, oil, 33 × 25½ in. Museu de Arte, Sâo Paulo

70 HEAD OF "VENUS VICTORIOUS"
(see 68)

71 THE BATHERS
1916, oil. Private collection, Paris

72 THE NYMPHS
About 1918, oil, 43¼ × 63 in. Louvre, Paris